Jackie -
Here's to having
more time to this
Thank you for
your support!
Love you!
Christine

Need More Time?

I CAN Help
Turn Busy into Productive

Christine Baker Marriage

Need More Time? I CAN Help
Copyright © 2017 by Christine Baker Marriage
ISBN- 978-0-9985506-6-4 (paperback)

No part of this publication may be reproduced, stored in a retrieval system, or transmitted in any form or by any means, electronic, mechanical, photocopying, recording, or otherwise without written permission of the Publisher.

For information regarding permission, write to:

The Zebra Ink
publisher@thezebraink.com
The Zebra Ink
3896 Dewey Avenue #196,
Rochester, NY 14616
www.thezebraink.com

Printed in the United States of America

Copyeditor: Robert Marriage
Cover Design: Susan Carmen-Duffy
Interior Formatting: Robert Marriage

Dedication

To my husband Rob, who has never stopped believing in me, never stopped supporting me, and has always pushed me beyond my limits.

To my amazing children, Jacqueline, Robert, Abby, Emily, and Michael whom without your schedules, interests and play dates, there would be no need to be this organized.

To all of my treasured loved ones that have gone before me, thank you for all that you have brought to my life. I know in time we will get to hang out again.

Acknowledgements

I sincerely thank Rob Marriage for his undying support and editing skills.

I am abundantly appreciative of Sheila Kennedy for her friendship, expertise and her amazing knack for pushing me past my boundaries.

I am beyond grateful for my sister Susan Carmen-Duffy who has been my biggest cheerleader, proofreader and cover creator! Please find her amazing work at CreateArt4Good.org.

A gigantic thank you to Michelle Frechette Ames who was able to capture me and my vision so easily in my images. Please find her amazing work at ClickHappyDesigns.com

Table of Contents

Dedication iii

Acknowledgements v

Table of Contents vii

Introduction 9

PART I 13

    Chapter 1: The Art of Being Busy 15

    Chapter 2: No One Has Time to Die 27

PART II 35

    Chapter 3: I CAN 37

    Chapter 4: I - Initiate Self Care 47

    Chapter 5: C - Create Unique Connections 55

    Chapter 6: A - Automate 63

    Chapter 7: N - Navigate your Plan 69

    Chapter 8: What happens if I CAN'T? 77

    Chapter 9: Final Thoughts 81

    Epilogue 83

Appendix 85

    A. I CAN Method 87

    B. What Are Your Priorities? 89

    C. Resources 91

    About the Author 93

Introduction

I bet I know something about you.

You are not a follower. You are a leader, a pioneer even. If you are reading this book then that tells me that you want to make your efforts more effective. It also tells me that you wish to create more opportunity in your life whether in business or at home. You, my friend, are paving the way for others, so those looking to you now for guidance and direction have a legacy to follow.

Okay that might be getting a little too deep right off the bat, but essentially that is what is happening. Any person who is looking to figure out how to be more effective and efficient with their time is going to be a go-getter, a thought leader, and someone who will do great things!

So, thank YOU for being here, reading this book and walking on this journey with me. I am really digging your company.

All systems are developed out of necessity and the one I am going to share with you is no different. I created this system - my secret recipe if you will - so that I could keep my business (and sometimes business**es**) and my family on track. At one point when I was writing this book I had three businesses and a family of seven. I have since pared things down a little bit to be true to my overall vision. Needless to say, I still have my amazing family of seven and now I have two businesses.

As you can imagine, my attention strays easily. I manage many things and many people at the same time. Willingly even. There were often times that I was so spun around though, I didn't know which way to go or what to try to accomplish first. That can be a death trap for anyone running a household or a small business. You can't get much done when you are frustrated, lost, and confused. In fact, some would say that it's wasting time swirling around like a lost puppy.

This system, my "secret recipe", serves two purposes:

1. Provides consistent motivation to the user.

2. Serves as a solid foundation - providing boundaries, connection stability, and direction so that you can tackle anything, either at home or in business.

You may ask yourself, "What on earth do those things have to do with anything?" I am so glad you asked. I promise to explain, but not until later. We need to go over a few other things first. But stick with me; I promise to get you there.

Have you ever noticed when people get overwhelmed or frustrated with the heavy load that life often gives us that they say, "I wish someone had given me a manual for this!" Exasperated, they search for ways to maneuver through uncertainty, hardships, and confusion.

This is true for both home and business. People are searching for a starting point, a reference point, a building block if you will, that they can always rely on, and always refer back to.

The principles in this book are the building blocks to that foundation. This book offers you the principles necessary to create prosperity, productivity and efficiency in any aspect of your life. These principles are applicable to any project, venture, life change, etc., that requires your attention and direction. After all we don't want to get lost and waste precious time.

PART I

Chapter 1: The Art of Being Busy

In order to find more time in your day and increase your productivity, you need to figure out how you are losing time.

What are you doing with your day? How are you setting yourself up for success? Are you setting yourself up to lose precious time by the choices you make or don't make?

Time efficiency is the key to how productive you are in your home life and personal life. Each aspect of your life (personal, home, work) has a role in how effective and efficient you are with your time. They all play into one another and affect the choices you make, the relationships you nurture, the paths you take, and ultimately how you spend your time. Having your personal, home, and work lives in balance is vital to your success. When there is an imbalance in any of them, it will spill over into other aspects of your life and will create chaos, confusion, feelings of being overwhelmed, and ultimately being lost.

I call this "functional coasting."

Most of the time we can still function and accomplish things, but in a survival, or superficial way - nothing meaningful, but we do get by. Before we know it, days, weeks, months, or even years have gone by and we have wasted SO. MUCH. TIME. It's embarrassing, disappointing and ultimately, we wind up asking ourselves, "How did we even get here?"

Functional Coasting, that's how.

I will also consider the argument that you have been "too busy" to choose otherwise. I frequently hear that as well. I maintain, however, that being too busy is simply another form of functional coasting. It is an excuse not to commit to a direction or a vision. It is a way to avoid real life and to simply survive. That is no way to live. You were born to thrive, not just survive. I believe that being too busy is a form of self-sabotage. It's avoidance at its most basic level.

When you are so busy that you are being pulled in more directions than your vision allows, you are not building your life you are sabotaging it.

You have ideas of who you want to be and things you want to do, but being "too busy" to accomplish them is just a huge lie. You CAN accomplish great things, do great things, be a great person and still have time on your hands. You don't have to be overworked and overwhelmed to feel purpose and success. Being busy is overrated and unnecessary.

I believe that there is a time and place for everything. There is enough time to spend with loved ones, to spend at work, to go on vacation, for playing with your children and friends, and to spend with customers and clients. You name it, you can find time for it, if it is that important.

Chapter 1: The Art of Being Busy

But you often forget how to manage that time. You throw all of your responsibilities into a mix and see where it winds up. It's so hard to decipher what is the best use of your time between lack of direction and the abundance of choices. The world you live in currently is so distracting.

To be honest and somewhat cliché, you only have so much time. No one knows quite how much, so to waste time seems frivolous. When you remember how short life is, you tend to not take it so much for granted.

When I was an adolescent and even into my teen and young adult years, being a busy person seemed like something to strive for. It meant you had purpose, worth and that people relied on you. At least this is what I convinced myself it meant.

I grew up in a wonderful home but my parents were always "busy." Too busy to play a game of cards with me or too busy to take me to a friend's house. Too busy to even have a friend over. I suppose looking back now that I convinced myself that being busy must be an important thing to be, because why else would my parents not want to spend time with me?

That might be a stretch and possibly a juvenile approach, but at the time I was convinced that my parents were very important people, and all of the work they did must have been equally as important. Don't get me wrong, they were important people to me and I was to them. Reality and day-to-day life however, gets in the way of our conceptual reality of time.

You always think you will have more time later in the day, or tomorrow or next week or next year. The problem is that other distractions enter into the equation and suddenly it is years later and those opportunities to share a game of cards or have friends over are gone. It's sad but it's reality.

I know now that being busy is not necessarily how I want to measure success, but that wasn't always the case.

There have been plenty of times in my life where I stayed busy, so I completely understand the concept. At certain times in my life, I am pretty sure I held the record for being in the top ten busiest people of all time. I used to be proud of how much I could manage. I stacked my day full of activities, to-dos, meetings, social lunches or visits. You name it; I tried to fit it in.

I was a stay at home mother of four children under eight years old. We made our own baby food, had a clean house with white carpets, and we made our own wrapping paper for every single holiday. Every. Single. One. I hosted and ran playgroups and mothers' groups. I brought my kids to the local preschool and became a teacher there without having any prior experience. In my "free time"- I trained myself, researched how to be a great preschool teacher and pored over other teachers' lesson plans. I refused to use the preschool's pre-existing lesson plans, because why not reinvent the wheel? I had it in my brain that in order to be

Chapter 1: The Art of Being Busy

taken seriously and to be influential to my class and colleagues, I had to come up with some amazing new lesson plan or concept. I was NOT about to use lesson plans that had already been done that were effective, that were tested, that worked and worked well. Why would I make my life easier? I longed for the opportunity to be busy. I thought reinventing the wheel would make me worthy, important and "busy." Instead it just made me exhausted and frustrated. It was a total waste of time.

Okay, lesson learned, or so I thought. I decided to reinvent another set of wheels! I volunteered to not only teach at Vacation Bible School, but to run the entire program. I got to a point where I took every opportunity that came across my desk for a chance to put myself out there as a contributor to the family or to society. I wanted to stay busy because I thought that is what people expected of me. I thought that is what would make me influential, important, and valued.

It was hard for me to find a balance between doing what was right for my family and also creating a space where I could process emotions, find myself, listen to my truth, and not feel guilty for doing so. Instead of having both, I decided to just do the best I could and prayed that it worked out.

I got married the October after college and had a baby that following spring. I never worked in the field that I went to school for (research psychology), instead I worked at my husband's family business as their receptionist. I was grateful for the earning potential and the opportunity to contribute to our upcoming bills. With that gratitude also came a feeling of failure. Failure to work in my major. Failure to not progress in a field that I had longed to break into since I was a young girl. It all seemed justified because I also wanted to be a mother. From the moment I heard I was pregnant, I instinctively gave up all of my intentions of being a doctor of research psychology and would devote 100% of my energy, thoughts, time, talents, and couple of kidneys if I had to, to be an out of this world mom and a fantastically spectacular wife.

I had high expectations of myself. Obviously.

Once I held my beautiful and healthy daughter in my arms, I never again thought about becoming Dr. Christine - Researcher Extraordinaire. I never gave up however on wanting to contribute and leave my mark on the world.

My husband and I decided that I would stay home and raise our daughter and whatever children came along after. Little did we know just how many children we would have (four together) or what life was going to offer us (lots of illnesses, surgeries and an untimely death).

I was totally committed to that decision, 100%. I wanted nothing more than to be a mom and to raise a family. My family was everything to me. I had few hobbies and when I did do something for myself, I felt guilty.

Chapter 1: The Art of Being Busy

No one told me how hard parenting would be, or if they did, I didn't listen. Looking back, I am sure I said something to the effect of, "Trust me. I know what I am doing." The truth of the matter was that I had no clue. I relied heavily on my instinct for most of the basics, but I struggled. Those feelings of struggle turned to feelings of being overwhelmed. Those feelings turned into depression. You can be depressed and high functioning, and that is what I was.

My "me time" was naptime. When I would close the door to my kids' rooms for naptime or quiet time, I would sing, *Oh Happy Day*. One time my son chimed back, "We can hear you and we are NOT happy."

I sang it much quieter from then on.

I recognized that I had a responsibility to my husband, to myself, and to our children to be the best care-giver I knew how to be. It was hard though, and I was tired. The only thing I knew how to do was to become busy. It is distracting, it is entertaining, and it allows you to numb your mind for a bit while you deal with your immediate necessities. That was my solution...keep the kids busy. If I could stay busy I would be able to avoid the reality that I was drowning and drowning fast.

Staying busy would serve so many purposes, I thought.

It would provide life experiences for the kids and me to cherish and remember forever.

It would wear them out so that early bedtimes would be possible.

It would keep my mind off the fact that I just wanted some basic time to myself and to be with other adults.

It would keep me from remembering that I still wanted to contribute as an individual. As Christine - not wife, mother, etc. Just little ol' me.

I want to mention here, in case you may be wondering where my husband was? Why wasn't he contributing more? My husband, Randy, was a gem, one in a million, but he was also the main breadwinner and felt obligated to work as hard as possible. To add to the situation, he worked with his brother and father in a family owned business where they all worked harder and longer than anyone else. To add even more to this story, he had cancer throughout our entire marriage. I can't remember how many times he was in and out of the hospital during our time together. It was really too many to count. Let's just say the older kids knew where all of the vending machines were in the hallways outside of the Emergency Department at our local hospital and where all of the good hiding spots were in the ED waiting room.

As we had more children, the desire to be something other than a caretaker and to participate, to give back, and to contribute something other than changing poopy diapers, surgical dressings, and math facts, grew stronger and stronger. I wanted to have validation of me as a human, me as Christine, not just as a mom or a wife or as a caregiver.

Chapter 1: The Art of Being Busy

There didn't seem to be any time for that so I just kept adding more responsibility to my plate so that I could become validated in other ways. I longed desperately for the kudos that comes from hearing "Job well done!" or "Your report came out great. Thank you!" I wasn't even sure what report I would or could write, but I did know that I wasn't writing any reports, so that must be what I was missing. Little did I know!

The only way I knew how I could achieve that was by being an out-of-this-world mom and a fantastically spectacular wife. I was that, and I managed it all.

That's just it: I managed it. I got by. I squeaked by. It wasn't living, it wasn't thriving. I was just surviving.

Being busy never fulfilled what I truly needed. Being busy was an opportunity to push away the guilt of wanting more out of life. Of wanting to thrive instead of just survive. I wanted to contribute as just me. Somehow, someway, I knew I would.

I now recognize that my parents were probably going through the same thing. Struggling to get by, struggling with depression, struggling with, "Is what I am doing creating value?"

When you keep yourself busy you often fail to notice opportunities for joy, balance, and pure freedom. You lose out on chances to live life. You wrestle with obligations and responsibilities like it's your job, because most of the

Part I

time it is. Don't get me wrong; there is a time and a place for working late to make a deadline. There are occasions where busy is appropriate and even acceptable. I am talking about the chronically busy. The people who can't say no to taking on more responsibilities. The people who bombard their schedules with obligations or business to seem important. The functionally coasting busy.

Obligations and Responsibilities are totally different friends.

Busy and Productive are not in the same friend group either.

Busy is a really close cousin to Avoidance.

Productivity is about priorities.

By sustaining a busy lifestyle, you create the illusion of importance, and of worth. It is much desired validation that you are needed in today's society through your talents, whatever they may be.

Being busy is a defense mechanism that keeps you from being truly present in the stillness of each day.

Busy also comes with guilt. You don't do enough. You don't contribute enough. You don't give of yourself enough. You don't _____ enough. You fill in the blank. Does this sound familiar?

Chapter 1: The Art of Being Busy

Productivity comes with satisfaction. That, to me, is success. No amount of money could be as satisfying as that pure moment where you know that you helped someone, touched someone, changed someone, just by doing "you" things - just by being you.

You don't have to be busy to be important. You just need to know how to balance it all. Balance is not about how much you can fit into a day without pulling your hair out. Balance is about choosing what to put into your day that serves you, your vision, and your goals.

If you want to figure out how you spend your time and what exactly your priorities are check out an exercise I included in the Appendix.

Chapter 2: No One Has Time to Die

"Time used well creates a lifetime of memories. Time used poorly creates a lifetime of regrets."
- Christine C. Baker Marriage

Why is it so important to worry about time management? Who cares?

Well, you should. Everyone should.

You only get a certain number of days to leave a legacy and to make your mark. Shouldn't you be purposeful with the time you do have?

You may think you have tons of time. You always think there is enough time, but some humans only get to live for minutes or even seconds, while others live for a hundred years. The truth is you never know. Another cliché, I realize, but it's true.

There has always been a spectrum of life experiences. Some people fit in the most remarkable experiences in a short amount of time while others wait for decades for the right time to do something remarkable, or to find happiness.

My experience has been that life is awfully short. Life has not been long enough for many people in my life. The one thing that I want more of from them is time together. I imagine that is true for many people.

If you are not happy in your current state, with your personal self, at home or at your work, then why are you still there? Why not work on changing what is not bringing you happiness?

Life it too short to be spent on crap that doesn't matter, doesn't serve your vision, or bring you joy.

Let me give you an example. It's a personal one, and typically I am uncomfortable about talking about it, but I believe it illustrates the point effectively.

Whether you want to believe it or not, you will come to a point in your life where you bargain for more

time - begging for another minute, hour, or day. You will do anything to have another chance at making the time you do spend mean more and last longer.

I had such a moment shortly after I turned 30. Life was good; remarkably boring at the time, even with four kids aged eight, six, two and one. I welcomed the boring, because up until then and for the previous ten years or so my life with my husband was a series of "survival pockets" mixed with regular everyday life. I call them "survival pockets" because either life was fantastic, normal and we were hitting our stride and thriving with a beautiful, normal family, or we were in crisis mode just trying to survive.

Chapter 2: No One Has Time to Die

He was sick most of the time and in and out of hospitals between treatments, surgeries and near-death experiences. Not the kind where you see the light, the kind where you are banging on death's door with a massive infection complete with pus oozing out of places it shouldn't be oozing out of. I too had my fair share of health issues mixed in with his. We were quite a pair.

Our love story was altogether remarkable. It starts out like a sweet Hollywood romantic movie where a boy, age 27, reluctantly goes to meet an equally reluctant girl, age 20, on a blind date. It quickly turns to love at first sight and they spend hours talking and learning as much as they can about each other. After the first date, the boy tells his mother that he just met the woman he is going to marry. (Insert the audience saying "Awwwww" track here.) Those first few hours together turn into days, then weeks and they both quickly realize that this relationship is here to stay.

So romantic, right?

The boy (my soon-to-be husband), and the girl (played by me), begin to build a life together and decide to marry. Baby number one comes the spring after we wed. The pregnancy had its ups and downs and all seemed to be going as expected. My husband, however, was sick more often than I was and we couldn't figure out what was the cause. We both assumed something benign probably due to stress, because he too kept a busy pace. After countless doctor visits and seven specialists, his last specialist finally decided to test him for cancer.

It was positive and not benign, but malignant. He was diagnosed at age 30 with Hairy Cell Leukemia. One of the rarest forms of cancer. Three people out of one million in America per year are diagnosed[1]. Just three and he was one of them.

For the next near seven years, we struggled together, grew together, and welcomed three more children into our hearts and home. He eventually had to have his spleen removed because that, too, was filled with cancer, not just his blood and his bone marrow. We knew that our growing old together may only be into our 40s or 50s, but we were dedicated to making it all work and doing the best that we could.

It wasn't perfect by any means. We had our spats, took each other for granted and we both felt underappreciated for all that we did. The bottom line however, was that we loved each other, our life, and our children. We would do anything for each other, even sacrifice all that we knew to be true to make the other happy.

With no spleen (and four germy kids), the emergency room visits were frequent and grew tiresome for both of us. He felt like a burden, and I felt helpless. It was a lot of coordination to get him to the hospital in time for the right

---

[1] https://www.hairycellleukemia.org/professionals/epidemiology/

Chapter 2: No One Has Time to Die

life-saving antibiotics, and also to coordinate someone to take and care of all four children for an undetermined amount of time. Each time we wound up in the hospital, I grew more and more fearful that this time might be the one where he doesn't come home. Each time he assured me by saying, "I don't have time to die."

The last trip to the hospital proved to test all that I knew about myself, my world, my faith and my love for him. We didn't make it in time for the life-saving antibiotics. The virus that had suddenly popped up turned to an infection. The infection then quickly turned septic. There was nothing that could be done.

At the young age of 30, I was given the most difficult task I had ever been asked to do; consider ending all artificial measures that were keeping my husband alive. I had to choose when time was over for him.

I convinced myself that if we only had more hours his health would take a turn for the better. People this young don't die, I thought. Surely time would be our savior and turn this situation around.

His organs began to shut down.

We just needed a little more time.

Surely his brain would understand that he wanted more time. That the children and I wanted more time with him.

That we needed him alive and somehow time would reverse the slow painful process of death.

The decision was made. There was no reason to keep his body alive any longer to ease my suffering or the suffering of our families. As the nurse began to shut the machines off, I convinced myself that somehow, someway, we would be granted more time. A miracle would happen and that Hollywood love story would not have to have a tragic end, leaving all of the movie-goers heartbroken and dissatisfied.

When the last machine turned off and there was no longer the blip of a heartbeat, time stood still. His time here on earth was complete. There was no more of it. The quantity was zero.

He was only 37. By anyone's expectation he should have lived another 50 years. He should have had more days, weeks, years. Decades even.

I found myself in the hallway outside of his room asking, "How did we even get here?"

He was feeling great earlier that week. In fact, he and I had a pretty life altering conversation that I will never forget. He was going to branch out of his job that he had had for the last 20 years - working for the family business - and pursue a business with his best friend.

They had a mutual passion and had decided to create a business out of it. He had planned to tell his dad and his

Chapter 2: No One Has Time to Die

brother the following Monday that he would phase out of the family business as this other endeavor took off and he hoped for their support. He was nervous about the conversation, but confident that this is what he wanted to do and more importantly, that it was time. I supported him 100%. This change was something that he was looking forward to, something that excited him and that he knew without a doubt would bring him joy.

That conversation never happened on Monday. He died instead.

I share this story with you, because Randy's time ran out. He was not able to pursue his vision or reach his goals. He was not able to see if this opportunity would make him happy.

I realized in the very moment he passed, that time is not merciful just because you beg and plead. Time really does come to an end for all of us. The Hollywood fairy tale ending would have to be revised, or so I thought. More on that a little later in the book.

I realized I had to make better use of the days I had left. It took a while but eventually I realized that it was time to stop being so busy. It was time to start creating a life for the kids and myself that Randy would be proud of. I knew then that pursuing something I did not feel strongly about was a waste of my time and energy. It was okay to still pursue my dreams. It was okay to thrive and not just survive.

You and I still have time, assuming I am still alive when you read this. You have right now to decide to take hold of your life and do what makes you happy. You have the privilege to use the time you do have to its fullest potential. Why would you waste it?

You don't ever have to say, "If only I had more time," because in reality you actually have it. You just have to learn to use the time wisely and with intense purpose.

What is stopping you from pursuing what brings you joy?

What is stopping you from starting that business?

What obligations are steering you away from your true calling?

What is preventing you from creating a business that is successful, or a home that is comfortable and thriving?

Is it because you think you have time?

Is it because you don't think you are worthy?

Is it because you are too busy?

The answer is you are never too busy to pursue what brings you joy. You are completely worth it and the time is now to make it happen. You CAN thrive and I am going to show you how.

PART II

Chapter 3: I CAN

Have you ever had those moments, days or maybe even longer where you are just filled with despair? Back in March of 2016, when I laid on my couch for nearly 6 weeks with influenza and then pneumonia that was the case for me. My doctor said it was the worst case of back-to-back illnesses she had seen in a long time, if ever. It was so bad that I couldn't even think about anything other than making it through the next hour, sometimes less than that…sometimes even just the next few minutes. I relied on the members of my family to care for themselves and my business. I knew systems were in place so that the business wouldn't totally shut down without me being there as much as I was before illness struck.

I remember I kept saying to myself:

> "You CAN make it through this."

> "You CAN survive."

> "Your business CAN survive also."

I have said that a lot in my life, always trying to be my own best cheerleader, to hopefully balance out the inner critic.

> "I CAN accomplish this."

> "I CAN make it through this."

> "I CAN make it to the end, just keep trying."

I find myself saying the same thing whenever I am encouraging friends or clients. "You CAN do it!" or "I believe you CAN do that!" Forever the optimist.

It is much more than that. There is a reason behind that specific type of phrasing, and I didn't quite realize it until early 2016, when I became very ill.

Up until then I often used the phrase because I appreciated the meaning behind the actual word. Dictionary.com defines the word "can" as to be able to; have the ability, power, or skill to.

When I say to someone, "You CAN do this.", I am saying that I believe that you are able to. I believe you have the ability to. I believe you have the power to. I believe you have the skill to do X, Y, or Z.

I mean it when I say it to others, and I don't say it lightly or casually. Naturally, I want people to do their best, but I am not going to tell someone that they can run for public office if their skill set makes them an excellent music teacher instead.

No, you really CAN'T do that. Sorry. You CAN'T be good at everything.

I used to think the word "can't" was an awful word. I didn't like it at all. I always took it as a challenge when someone would say to me, "You CAN'T do that."

Chapter 3: I CAN

I have a perfect example and what started this whole thought process to begin with.

Believe it or not, it started when I was 8. My godparents who lived just down the street came over for dinner. This wasn't a rare occurrence as we were close not only in proximity but we also had a close relationship. They were my parents' best friends, but felt like family.

I remember a certain dinner, in particular, because of the conversation. My Godfather was taking a new job with a larger company and would be moving out of state. My father had just been promoted in his job as well, so there was a lot of talk about careers and moving up and creating a better life for their respective families. I was the youngest of my parents' children and at the time: my brother was in the military, and my sister had just gotten married. My Godparents' children were also all grown and out of the house. Needless to say, I was odd man out and was often included in many adult conversations. Nothing inappropriate, but to an eight-year-old kid, how to manage editors for a major newspaper company or how the new shipment of gaskets that came in were a 1/8 inch off in size was not my type of stimulating conversation. In an effort to include me in that conversation, my Godfather turned to me and said ...

"So, what do you want to do when you grow up?"

I could feel the answer coming from the tips of my toes. I was nervous. I felt silly and unsure of what might come out of my mouth. Finally, I let the answer burst out!

"EVERYTHING! I want to do everything!"

My parents and godparents exchanged a glance that for an eight-year-old felt just as long as waiting to be picked last for dodgeball in Physical Education. Maybe longer. In reality it was probably only a half of a second, but after their eyes locked they all burst into roaring laughter. I suddenly felt like the butt of a joke on Rowan and Martin's Laugh-In, and not in a good way.

They were laughing at me and my obvious silliness. I was so embarrassed.

My Godfather followed up my response with, "Oh honey…You can't do everything." The heat and humiliation that came over me was almost too much and I came very close to running out of the room.

But I didn't. I stayed.

The same from-the-toes gumption that came just moments earlier prompted my response to him and with tears in my eyes, I replied,

"Oh, yes I CAN! Watch me."

Needless to say, I was sent to my room and the once celebratory dinner for the five of us, quickly turned into a

Chapter 3: I CAN

whispered conversation in the living room between the remaining four adults and me sitting on my bed left to "think about what I've done."

What is curious to me is that this word "CAN", that I used in my response, is so insanely powerful. It is truly motivational. It has brought me through ALL of my darkest times and ALL of my triumphs.

I became a widow at age 30 with four kids under eight.

Did I feel helpless? Yes.

Did I feel lost and alone? You bet.

Was I terrified and uncertain as to what my future held? Absolutely.

But I pulled myself up, and I told myself over and over again, "You CAN do this." And I did. My children are nearly all grown now and THRIVING. I don't think I could be more proud of them.

In 2007, I graduated school as a licensed massage therapist and sat for the New York State licensing Boards. I had begun school in early 2006 and was thrilled to finish nearly top of my class (a doctor and nurse beat me in the student ranking). Going to school five days a week and raising a family simultaneously was challenging, but feasible because I had already begun to put some of these time saver methods in place. I passed my boards and began a private massage therapy practice. Don't get me wrong, I had tremendous support from loved ones, but none of this would have been possible had I not employed the power of I CAN.

In 2013, I started a wellness center in my hometown. As a New York State Licensed Massage Therapist, I witnessed countless people struggle with their health and wellness that needed complementary care to their traditional healthcare. Not many facilities offered complimentary services, so I decided that I wanted to do just that. My goal was to be the best in my city. I wanted to be voted Rochester's best wellness center, and seven months later, I accomplished just that. Why? Because I told myself over and over, "You CAN do this!".

"By saying I CAN, you are empowering yourself to believe in your infinite capabilities."
- Christine C. Baker Marriage

This teeny tiny phrase, I CAN, is the basis of my "secret sauce" to productivity and success. It is that powerful.

Let me explain what I mean.

I have been in several different situations in my life, traveled many places, and worn many hats. This has truly fed my favorite hobby as an avid people watcher. I studied people instead of gambling when I was in Las Vegas. I had

Chapter 3: I CAN

so much more fun and hardly spent a dime! I have had the opportunity to observe and learn from people from all walks of life. I listen to what their joys and angsts are in both life and in business. There is a common theme throughout.

Over the years, I have discovered four "typical" reasons why the structure of businesses and the structure of families fail. I say typical because every situation is different. With each different personality and circumstance comes a different joy or angst that may not be typical. For arguments sake, I will contest that if you can create solutions (which of course I have) for these "typical" issues, then you can create a solid foundation and set yourself up to handle whatever special problems or accomplishments come your way.

Activities that lead to Structural Breakdown in Home/Business

- Burnout
- Lack of unique connection to your customers or clients
- No systems in place
- No direction or action plan

So how does that translate into my "secret sauce?" I promise to go into much deeper detail in the following chapters, and of course offer you a strategy to help you succeed. But think about it. Have you had an experience where one of these was not the ultimate cause of the breakdown? I know I haven't. I can trace every one of my structural breakdowns to one of these underlying reasons. What happens is that when problems arise and we don't have a solid foundation in place, we experience shame, guilt, and fear of judgement from others.

I have had several businesses in my life. Looking back on all of them and with the understanding of these core issues, I recognize the problems with each of them. I have had a few failed relationships and again, I can completely understand where they went wrong. I should throw in this disclaimer that I am a believer of the notion that everything happens for a reason. That being said, I do believe that the mistakes you make, you are created to make them so that you might learn from them, grow with them, and be better on the other end. That is what I am trying to help you do. Get to the end faster. You will still make mistakes as you proceed through your life and business, but having a foundation to fall back on will get you much further ahead and will ultimately speed up the learning process.

Getting back to the reasons for structural failure in home or in business.

Once you learn this motivational management system, you will be able to pick yourself up out of being overwhelmed and frustrated. Maybe that feeling of "What on earth am I doing?" will go away once and for all.

Chapter 3: I CAN

You will now be able to say I AM capable. I CAN kick some ass today. I CAN do this.

That is why I named the system, the...

I CAN Method.

I love acronyms. Remember the planet one? "My Very Educated Mother," etc.

Well that is what I did with this system. I wanted to incorporate something that was easy to remember, something to keep me motivated, something to keep me focused and also managing the top four aspects of business and life where most people are deficient.

Let's take another look at the top four reasons why entrepreneurs and small businesses continue to struggle especially within the first few years and why relationships continue to fail.

1. Burnout
2. Lack of unique consistent connection to your customers or clients
3. No systems in place
4. No direction or action plan

To avoid burnout:

I = INITIATE SELF CARE

To avoid a lack of unique consistent connection to your customers or clients:

C = CREATE A UNIQUE CONNECTION

To avoid not having any systems in place:

A = AUTOMATE

To avoid not having a direction or action plan:

N = NAVIGATE TO SUCCESS

See the acronym? **I. C.A.N.**

Pretty awesome, right?

Let's dive in a little deeper.

Chapter 4: I - Initiate Self Care

Whatever you do, DO NOT skip over this chapter. Self-Care is often a scary or non-existent concept to people. It is vital to the success of everything. It is the first layer of the foundation to your productive, successful, time finding self.

So often in your lives and in your business, you put yourself last. You think you have time at the end of the day or the week. Maybe you can sneak some time into the weekend or take a day off by the end of the month, just to catch up.

But that time never actually comes. Those moments you hope to sneak in never actually happen. It is imperative to carve out time to get things done, to live life, to work on your business, whatever you need to do. Self-care is no different.

Taking care of yourself is never a bad thing. You actually waste time by not taking care of yourself.

Your body yearns, and I do mean *yearns*, for balance. The actual scientific term is homeostasis. Homeostasis is your body's natural way for creating balance or equality within your internal environment all the while dealing with external stimulation. When you are in balance, your body is in a state of "ease." When your body is out of balance, it is in a state of "dis-ease." That looks A LOT like Disease! Pretty cool, right?

Let me throw a little more physiology at you before I connect all of the dots.

The autonomic nervous system is the part of the central nervous system responsible for control of the bodily functions not consciously directed, such as breathing, the heartbeat, and digestive processes[2].

When you are living in a state of dis-ease, your brain, more specifically your autonomic nervous system, receives a signal that your body or a part of your body is in a state of distress. That signal initiates the fight-or-flight response, which releases hormones into your system to cope with the perceived external threat that is causing the distress. The external activity that is causing stress could be actual danger like a car accident or it could be lack of sleep, which also causes a hormonal imbalance.

I know what you must be thinking. I will NEVER be in balance. Don't get discouraged, because while that is somewhat true, you have the power to work towards balance through self-care!

When you become tired, stressed or even ill, that is your body's way of slowing you down so that you can take notice and initiate self-care. Your body will stop you at all costs to get your attention. It will create a pause for you to slow down, and when those things happen it is a wakeup

---

[2] https://www.britannica.com/science/autonomic-nervous-system

Chapter 4: I - Initiate Self Care

call. Time to slow down, to reevaluate, to rest. You often see it as an inconvenience instead of the blessing that it is.

As a former bodyworker (NYS Licensed Massage Therapist) I would hear a lot of excuses from my clients about their lack of self-care.

"I will sleep when I'm dead."

You actually won't sleep at all. You will be dead. Sleep works to restore your body's natural state of homeostasis. Your body automatically goes into a restorative state to help you be a better you the next day. There is only one problem ... you have to actually go to sleep and sleep for seven to eight hours. If you have trouble sleeping, try to figure out why and solve those issues. Create the opportunity for your body to get back to balance.

This excuse from clients is my favorite.

"I don't have time for self-care. I'm too busy."

So many of you think that taking care of yourself is luxurious, something wonderful you will get to eventually or an extravagant treat. Well, you're partially correct. It can be luxurious and it can be extravagant, but then it crosses the line that is in between self-care and self-indulgence. I think this is the argument: What one person may call self-indulgent, another would call self-care. I think the point is to do it, not to judge it right? Let's just go with the understanding that whether you decide to have a massage at a high-end spa with fluffy robes, slippers that make your toes feel as cozy as walking on cotton balls and special chocolates from chocolatiers that I can never pronounce, or if you decide to receive a massage at a wellness center with dimmed lights, serene music and focused energy, it's still a massage. You just decide how extravagant you want to make it.

As a former body worker, I prefer less fluff and more stuff, meaning I want my body worker to focus on me, my muscles, and the "issues in my tissues" - not if my robe is ready or if my water has the correct ratio of cucumbers to mint leaves in it. I personally don't care about that stuff. That doesn't add to my self-care. I can create my own infused water, but again, that is just me. You may think differently and that is okay. The point is to actually think about it, explore what you consider self-care and weed out what doesn't serve you.

Deciding to take care of you is by far the hardest decision to make. You are choosing to put yourself first. You live in a society where people who consciously put themselves first are seen as selfish, self-centered and egotistical. Western culture is constantly calling for you to do for others, serve others, and be MORE for others.

How can you give more, do more, and be more when you are burned out?

You can't and you don't have to. It's that simple.

Chapter 4: I - Initiate Self Care

Self-Care Suggestions

If you go through your day and are saying - "I need a break!" - that is your body crying out for you to take care of it. So, take that break and build in some consistent self-care.

1. **Set a standing appointment with yourself.** You don't break appointments with your clients, customers, or children, so why would you dare to break one with yourself? Show yourself the same respect you show others.

   I cannot recommend this tip enough. Set a standing appointment with yourself at whatever interval you are comfortable with. You can take some time daily for 15-30 minutes or you can make a whole day of it once a month. It is whatever works for you, your schedule and your comfort level. The idea is that the more you take care of yourself, the more you will want to. The 30 minutes a day won't seem so daunting, and more like a balancing slice of heaven, if you are consistent. I schedule a day once a month where I go off the grid. No phones, no schedule, no social media and no one knows where I am. I get giddy when I know the day is approaching. I am a better overall person because of it.

2. **Eat to nourish your body not to suppress it**. I am NOT a dietician at all but I do know that eating foods that are not healthy for you contribute to the

dis-ease of your body. Eating whole foods that nourish you, contributes to your health and overall balance. When your physiological processes are working well, the closer you will be to creating a homeostatic environment in your body.

3. **Sleep.** It is vital to human survival.

4. **Date yourself.** Take yourself out on a date. Get dressed up, plan it all out and then follow through with it. Try new things. Explore. Ramble. Get lost! Be creative! How do you know what you will like to do for self-care if you don't explore your options?

5. **What are your ideas?**

One of the top reasons why businesses fail and why families fall apart is burn out. You just cannot and should not keep up with a hectic, unreasonable schedule. There are only 24 hours in the day! To maximize your efforts and receive the maximum benefits, your day's responsibilities can be divided into three categories.

A. Personal

B. Home

C. Business/Work/School

Each category gets eight hours per day. Not as easy as it sounds, and I recognize that. Again, it is all about balance.

Chapter 4: I - Initiate Self Care

If you are working 10 hour shifts for four days which takes time away from the personal and home allotted hours, then make sure those three days off you are spending more time on home and personal time. You have the power to create an equal, balanced environment.

There has to be self-care involved or our bodies will slow us down so we can get back to balance. Your body is constantly striving for balance. Self-care is completely subjective and encompasses a huge array of activities. At some point every day you have to draw the line in the sand and say enough is enough and let the focus fall onto you.

Read a book. Take a walk. Watch a funny show or video. Whatever makes you happy - DO IT.

If you don't take care of yourself, you won't be able to show up and be fully present to any celebration or crisis. You will be dragging, confused, irritated, and less you! The connections you create will be less meaningful and more superficial because the real you is not showing up. The real you wants to take a nap! Take that nap, then you will be ready to create those unique connections.

Chapter 5: C - Create Unique Connections

Another way to increase the quality of each day and decrease the amount of time wasted is through human connection. It is essential for life. According to an article in Psychology Today[3], one of the top reasons why relationships fail is because people don't make relationships a priority. People are becoming more distant, leading separate lives and not able to find common ground on even the most mundane tasks and responsibilities.

It is true in business as well. Customers are walking away from "one and done" companies because they are instead looking for a connection to the person or business they are buying from. They want a story or a unique way of connecting to that entity where they are placing their money.

So how are you showing up to your relationships, whether personal or professional? You hear it all the time when you are in business. How do you set yourself apart from the competition? So, I will ask the same question. How do you set yourself apart? It doesn't have to be just in the professional sense but at home as well.

How do you stand out?

---

[3] https://www.psychologytoday.com/blog/the-mindful-self-express/201503/the-top-4-reasons-relationships-fail

How do you share yourself in a way that is different and creates an impression?

How do you communicate to your loved ones? Your clients? Your colleagues?

You weren't born to fit in or be ordinary. You were born to be exactly who you are and that is enough. No more, no less. When you try to hide yourself, and mainstream your personality, quirks, and what makes you unique, then it has the opposite effect. You go unnoticed.

What a complete waste of time.

You have a unique fingerprint on this world. And that will be what connects you to the right people. Hiding who you truly are in order to be more "mainstream" disconnects your authenticity from others. It's the authentic, real people that you remember.

I have been shopping at the local grocery store near my home for 15 years. I always get the same deli meats and rarely vary my selection. There are two people that are usually working the time of day that I am shopping. I have no idea what their names are but I do know this about them:

- Employee #1 is female and has a nasty attitude. She rolls her eyes whenever I ask to have my ham sliced so thin it's almost shaved. I am not a fan of her.

Chapter 5: C - Create Unique Connections

- Employee #2 is male and has a great attitude most of the time. He is tall and always calls me honey instead of Ma'am. I like him.

These two have been working at the deli counter for as long as I can remember. I do not know their names. I do not know anything about them. Nothing remarkable stands out when I think about them, and I don't usually think about them at all. If I never saw them again, I would most likely forget they were ever in my world to begin with.

Now let me tell you about Mike. I met Mike a few weeks ago while grocery shopping. Mike has worked for the local grocery store's Deli Department for 27 years. He has four grandchildren and his neighbor likes the same deli meat as I do and cut in the same manner…shaved. Except, she (his neighbor) puts hers in a tortilla, with a little bit of cream cheese, a little bit of mayo and a dollop of mustard, yep - he said "dollop." That is how she gets her kids to eat all of those things together. Now on special occasions she will throw in some nice thin slices of swiss cheese.

I learned all of that in four minutes! He greeted me with the biggest smile. He connected a product I liked to something valuable that I could use (his neighbor's recipe). He was personable and authentic. He offered me a unique connection. How we interacted told me who he was and how he was as a person: dynamic, giving, cheerful. Don't you know that as I was finishing up my shopping, I gathered all of those ingredients and made it for my kids the next day? They loved it as well! Now when I go grocery shopping, I make sure to stop by the deli counter on the days that Mike is working and wait for him to be available. He offered me a way to get to know him, like him and trust him. The other ones ... I still don't know their names. Actually, I take that back. Employee #1 is "eye rolling lady" and Employee #2 is "super nice tall man." Might be too long for the name tags, but it works for me.

Mike wasn't afraid to be judged, or mocked, or afraid to share his story. Mike was okay with being himself and creating a unique connection. He was 100% present. He has my attention and my deli meat order from now on.

You are taught that in order to get someone to buy a product or service from you that you need to touch them 7-10 times and now even up to 21 times before people even buy from you. Don't you want to make the first few times as impactful as possible? Don't you want to make them count instead of struggling to still get their attention at time 21?

You remember that kid in high school that had a blue mohawk, right? Don't be afraid to be that kid. You don't have to dye your hair, but you do have to be who you are. Be authentic. Be you. Be real.

If people can't or won't work with you because of your uniqueness, then you don't want them as friends or customers anyway. There will always be people for you if

Chapter 5: C - Create Unique Connections

you are true to yourself. Don't put any more time into being ordinary. People don't remember or care about ordinary, they remember pure and real.

There is another aspect to creating a unique connection that I want talk about here that didn't really occur to me until I started writing this book. I have shared this sentiment myself many times, especially when people pass away and that is that I wish I had more time with them.

We long for more time with our loved ones after they pass away. We wish there was more time with our children at a certain age (usually young).

We want more time with our friends.

"That was such a great time, we should do that again." is what usually gets said.

Do you really want the additional time? Maybe. I think ultimately you are impressed by the unique connection that you just experienced, and are impressed by the quality of time you have created within that time.

> Time is of the essence...
>
> Time is fleeting...
>
> Time is short...
>
> I wish I had more time!

How many have you heard or said? I know I have said them all several times! It's imperative to remember that these clichés are said over and over again to spark inspiration, to motivate us to take action. You try and spread the importance of using your time wisely through these clichés.

These are wonderful sentiments, true, and the people expressing them have great intentions. They want that connection; they want to be productive. I am telling you that this will never happen unless you change your mindset.

The mindset is that you want quantity over quality. You want more time and more of this and that opportunity and more of whatever, but the reality is that what you truly seek is **quality** over quantity.

Every single person gets the same number of hours in any given day. Life can be longer for some than for others, but that is quantity. It's about the quality of how you spend your time that matters.

"It's not about the quantity, it's about the quality."

- Christine C. Baker Marriage

Relationships come and go. Your health and wellness comes and goes. Money ebbs and flows. Time is the only finite product in your life. You cannot manipulate the variable to extend it. I have already tried that several times and it never works.

Create Unique Connections at Home

1. **Set aside time to share with each person in your household, individually**. Set a recurring monthly date for a walk, to share an ice cream, or a full-on date.

2. **Reach out to loved ones that you don't see often on a regular basis**. A short phone call, a note left on a mirror or pillow, a quick "thinking of you" text or email or a pop-in visit are excellent ways to stay connected and to let them know how much you think of them.

3. **Be accessible as often as your boundaries will allow**. It's okay to set boundaries surrounding how available you are to your family, but be reasonable. Recognize when your family/friends may need you more than your work or phone needs you.

4. **Share your signature delight.** Do you have a unique treat that you share to let others know that you think they are pretty special? It could a special culinary treat or something creative for a birthday, an accomplishment, a special day at school.

5. **What are your ideas?**

Create Unique Connections in Business

1. **When connecting with customers and clients, always stay true to your mission and message.**

2. **Create an interaction that is unforgettable.**

3. **Consistently build the relationship. Business relationships are no different than those with your family and friends.** Nurture them on a regular basis with dependable connections.

4. **Send really great emails.** My friend Sharon always sends me fantastic, dynamic emails. It is as if I am reading a conversation that she is having with me and only me. It makes me feel special and as if she is really considering my needs with regards to her business.

5. **Be unique and authentic on Social Media.** Whatever platforms you utilize for promoting yourself professionally, make sure your extraordinary personality shines through so when people see a post, they know it's you!

6. **What are your ideas?**

Chapter 6: A - Automate

Anything that has ever grown in business has been because of automation. Systems can be created and automated so you can spend more time being creative. Entrepreneurs are naturally creative people, who need time to explore, research, and experiment. Reinventing the wheel on vital business processes only drags us down and kills the vibe. Am I right? So, having automated, regulated, formulated systems in place takes the guesswork out of that mundane, but essential, structure, and allows the creative entrepreneur or overworked parent to be successful.

The automation of processes is actually more natural than you think. Most systems in our bodies are already automatic: digestion, dilation of our pupils, breathing, even vomiting (not my favorite automatic process but it's a good one just the same).

Routines, once we learn them, become automated. You have routines for your morning and evening. Driving to and from work becomes automatic to the point where you may have found yourself driving to work on a non-work day. Your body creates a habit by making those movements over and over again.

Our minds and bodies have automated each of these processes. You no longer have to put conscious thought toward the actions, because your brain has learned the action to create the desired outcome.

Your bodies and your minds naturally know and understand that in order to survive, you need to learn and learn quickly. You actually automate as much as possible so you can maintain a steady lifestyle.

You gravitate toward automation naturally. It's natural to try and create systems that will help you be more productive and execute actions with as much efficiency as possible. When you don't utilize automation, you create more work for yourself. It's reinventing the wheel. If it has already been done for you, you don't need to put the time and effort into creating a new one.

I used to believe that I needed to reinvent the wheel in order to put my mark on whatever I was doing. As you learned in the last chapter, you automatically do that by being as authentic as possible. By not utilizing processes that have a proven track record from efficiency you are wasting time. The key to counteract that is to automate as much as you possibly can. Often you don't use automated processes because you fear that you will become more of a "vanilla box," but the opposite is true. By using automated processes, you will then have more brain space, energy, and creativity to put toward your work, your life and your relationships. When you are able to look at something in a new light, you have a refreshing change.

You can automate almost everything now. With modern technologies such as our smart phones, tablets, apps and coordinating websites, there is no reason not to automate.

My all-time favorite online application is ToDoist.com. I have tried nearly all of the online to do list apps and I always come back to this one. It has a mobile version as well and it all syncs nicely together. I love this for daily or weekly recurring tasks that I don't want to have to write down constantly, or quarterly and yearly tasks that I know I just won't remember.

Some people still love paper automation. The feel of a new yellow legal pad connecting to your favorite pen. There is nothing like a new list cascading down the lines of the fresh sheet of paper.

In case you hadn't noticed, I am one of those people who LOVES LOVES LOVES paper. I can't help it. I remember things better when I write them down.

I love my routine, because it helps me automate certain aspects of my life. I can spend less energy on those tasks, knowing that they will take care of themselves because there is a certain "protocol" that my time and energy are no longer a contributing factor for its success.

Automation Suggestions

1. **Daily Check In.** Ask yourself, is this task that I am doing something that I can automate? Is it something that I can create as a repetitive task in my planner or on Google Tasks or a to do list? Taking the time to create that system may seem daunting at first but once it is done ... it is done. That time can

now be allocated elsewhere in your business or home. Another way to look at it is, if you are doing the task daily or even on a semi-regular basis, it should be automated.

2. **Write a To Do List.** It can be daily, weekly, monthly, quarterly or yearly. What is important is that it works for you. I actually have all of the above for certain tasks. I don't have to change my furnace filter weekly, so I schedule it quarterly.

3. **Keep your To Do List in a journal type notebook or binder.** There is nothing worse that losing your to do list. Have you heard of bullet journaling, chronicle journaling or binder journaling? I have done all three and explain it in more detail on my website. This type of task automation is what keeps me on track for both home and business. It saves my sanity! I can't wait to share all about it! You can find more information about it on my website: http://ccbakermarriage.com/complimentary/

4. **Create a morning and evening routine.** This is mine:

Home/Morning:

- Stretch/Exercise
- Read/Meditate/Pray (whatever grounds you)
- Get washed up and dressed

- Prepare meals for the day
- Conquer your to do list

Home/Evening:

- Stop working by a certain time every night
- Declutter your mind by jotting down ideas or tasks for the next day
- Stretch
- Wash up and dressed for bed
- Ground yourself again through meditation, reading, yoga or simply by being still

Business

- Check your to dos
- Check your contact portals (email, phone, social media, postal mail) for messages
    - Respond as soon as you can as appropriate
    - Carve out adequate time to accomplish all of your tasks that are to be done today
- Crush it!

5. **What are your ideas?**

Chapter 7: N - Navigate your Plan

I venture to guess that even though you have a plan, it doesn't always go the way you expect it to. I have been there. I think we all have. Flexibility is a must have for sure. The path you plan for may not be the one you ultimately take, so it is important to remember the end game. What do you ultimately want to work toward? In the end, it doesn't matter how you get there as long as you do it with integrity, and as ethically, responsibly as possible. Ultimately you need to do what serves you and your life the best.

Trust that whatever you do you will wind up exactly where you are supposed to be. Having a plan in place for business or your personal life is the last ingredient to my "special sauce" for success. You CAN reach your destination so much easier if you have a clue as to where you are going and how you may want to get there.

Case in point:

My brother and his beautiful family have lived in Virginia for over 25 years. We travel the 10-hour trip about once a year, sometimes more. I know how to get there and back. I am able to tell you where the good gas stations are located, the good eateries to stop at, and where all of the clean rest stops are along the way to and from my home. I no longer need a map. I do not need a GPS. I am fully aware of the

Part II

quickest route to get there and back. One might argue that the trip is automated now.

Several years ago, my then husband decided that on a return trip home from seeing my brother and his family, we were going to take a different route home. He said he grew bored of the typical route and wanted to take a different way home. Now this idea had great potential. Had we done things the right way we could have had an amazing adventure. Instead it turned into a disaster.

Imagine, if you will, a small sedan packed to the rim with suitcases, diaper bags, a pack-and-play, a cooler, countless toys, blankets, etc. We packed everything you needed to have for an 18-month old and an infant - a breastfeeding infant even. When I asked how we were getting home, he responded, "I figured I would just head north."

Those were not the directions I was used to and not the answer I was looking for. It was by far the WORST trip of my life. We ran into a horrific snow storm. Diapers ran out about two-thirds of the way home and we couldn't find a convenience store to purchase more. We wound up in Trenton, New Jersey which is nowhere near where we lived. Hours later, we wound up in Trenton again. I am not even joking. Nineteen hours later we finally made it home.

We did make it home, but not without many arguments, much frustration and many scary moments of slipping and sliding on icy roads. The point of the story is we should have mapped out our journey before we ventured into

Chapter 7: N - Navigate your Plan

uncharted territory, mapped out benchmarks, laid out places to stop and reevaluate. There still would have been a snowstorm, but we could have made arrangements for hotel accommodations if needed. We could have also said, "when we get to this point of the trip, we can hop back on the route we know especially if this one isn't working."

It was a total travel bomb, but we learned so much. Stick with your original plan. Go with your gut instinct and keep your eye on the destination.

The other side is you can get overzealous with your plans and plan every step and get upset when you don't hit the mark in YOUR time. The ideal situation is to have flexibility and appreciate that at any moment things could go not as planned. You need to be able to say, "things will work out; I am still reaching my goal; I am still getting to where I need to be."

Check in on what you are doing and ask yourself, "Am I following my dreams?"

Do you really want to have that many more hours to manage or do you just not know what you are doing in those hours, so you meander due to lack of planning?

Are you being efficient in those hours?

I wish someone could do this for me. I don't have time for me.

Is it that or that you don't have ways of automating your time?

Do you know where you are headed?

Do you have that endgame in mind and all of the possible plays ready?

I'm going to be honest … I am not a huge fan of business plans. I am more of an action plan kind of a girl, which is similar to business plans only there is more doing, than projecting. Not having any plan is the same as sitting in the middle of the ocean watching the world go by.

Here are a few suggested questions to help you evaluate how well you are planning.

1. **What is your overall vision?**

Chapter 7: N - Navigate your Plan

2. **What are you planning for and why is it important?**

3. **What are the goals you need to accomplish in order to see your vision actualized? Be as detailed as you need to be. You may want to transfer this eventually to an actual journal or word document so you can track your progress.**

4. **What actions do you take each day that keep you on track, that keep you on the road that you are navigating as that pioneer? Remember, as a pioneer you are probably doing this blind, as you are the one creating the trail.**

5. **What are you doing to make sure you have the destination in sight?**

6. **Are you checking in with your goals? How often?**

7. **Are you creating ways to build your business, your team, your network? What are they?**

8. **Are you checking with yourself to see if you have knowledge and skills to pursue a certain route or opportunity? Are there any that you have identified that could be pursued?**

9. **Is what you are doing today getting you closer to where you want to be tomorrow?**

10. **What is in your schedule that is not serving you? How can you turn that around so that your schedule is working for you and not against you?**

11. Are you being intentional with your time? Are you using your time purposefully?

[There are so many more suggestions for self-care, creating unique connections, automation and navigation to talk about. I do so on a continual basis in my blogs on my website, so check them out and see if any of the suggestions resonate with you.]

This navigation skill will keep you focused and on target and out of the typical expected start up business and relationship failure statistics.

Being a contributing human is hard. Not having a clear direction of where to begin or what direction to go in is even harder. You CAN do this. Implementing the I CAN Method into your daily business life will transform your confusion to connectivity, lead you from dismay to direction, and propel your day into productivity.

Chapter 8: What happens if I CAN'T?

Before I end, let me ask you this ...

What happens when you recognize you CAN'T do something?

Is it failure? No.

When you discover that you are no longer able to give your time and energy to something to make it successful that is when you ...

T...Terminate your efforts. By terminating your efforts, you then free up time and energy for the things you are good at. Everyone is good at something but you don't have to be good at everything.

"Even though we are capable of anything we put our minds to, doesn't mean we have to do them all. We must choose to do what will bring us closer to our vision and goals."
- Christine C. Baker Marriage

Ask yourself, will this activity, job, project, trip, or relationship bring me closer to accomplishing my goals and realizing my vision? If the answer is no ... then DON'T DO IT. A simple "No, thank you." will do. No explanation needed. Remember to serve you first, so that you can serve others.

I think the word CAN'T is just as powerful as the word CAN. There is power in knowing what your strengths and weaknesses are. There is true wisdom in knowing what you are capable of and where you can use some assistance.

To me, when I hear the phrase, "I CAN'T!", I immediately think of those in my life (whether business or home) who CAN. Those people that come to mind then become my Team. Instead of can't having a surrendering connotation, instead of it meaning terminate, it is simply a call for action.

T = TEAM

If you network (and you all should at some point in your career), then hopefully you have built up a "team" of professionals that you CAN trust, that you CAN rely on and that you CAN bring aboard your activity, job, project, trip, relationship, etc. Knowing where your strengths lie, and pursuing them full force is what is going to make you a better business owner and parent. Recognizing where your efforts need to be terminated, seeking out others who are good at those efforts, and making them part of your team is what is going to make you a successful, productive person.

It's okay to say no. It's not a bad word. Can't is not a bad word either.

Deciding to terminate your fruitless efforts or delegate actions to your team contributes to your overall time productivity. Knowing what your capabilities are is an asset. It allows you the freedom to focus on expressing and developing your expert capabilities. In knowing what your limits are, you also create opportunity for those in your "team" to develop their capabilities. To have the strength to say you can't do something is never a failure, but rather a chance you give others to shine in their greatness; freeing up you to shine in yours. Be proud of your limitations, for they CAN and will help you thrive.

Chapter 9: Final Thoughts

When you choose to be frivolous with your time, you also choose the rat race. You choose to consciously waste opportunity. You choose to consciously be disorganized and not true to yourself.

When you consciously choose to manage your time so that you are efficient and effective, you are validating the value of your time. When you treat your time as desirable and not dispensable, you become your best authentic self, validated in purpose and productivity instead of maintenance and busyness.

Whichever path you decide to take, whatever way you decide to raise your family, whichever business or career you choose to engage in, you CAN do this! You CAN be a successful, productive thriving person and not a busy, exhausted, surviving human.

> *You weren't born to just survive.*
>
> *You were born to thrive.*
>
> *You weren't born to be anonymous.*
>
> *You were born to make a difference.*
>
> *You were born to uniquely contribute to humanity. That isn't a religion thing; it's a human thing.*

There are many ways to make better use of your time. I have shared strategies that you can employ instantly that help create more hours in your day and make those 24 hours seem richer, more fulfilled, deeper, more productive and your relationships more meaningful.

I believe that you are capable of creating quality time in your day. You are capable of spending more time with your customers, your families and friends, and with yourself. I believe that rich human connection is the seed of all powerfully useful creativity.

Implementing the I CAN Method into your daily life will transform your confusion to connectivity, lead you from dismay to direction and propel your world into productivity.

Great leaders or pioneers don't start out to be great leaders at all, they start out wanting to make a difference. It's not about the role, it's about the goal. Whatever your goal is - whatever difference you choose to make - **I believe in you.** I know you CAN do it and I look forward to watching you.

Thank you for reading this. I believe in this work and I would love to be able to help you more. Feel free to email me at success@ccbakermarriage.com and let me know how I can help you find more time.

These ideas that I have shared are my own and based on my own experiences. Life is a journey, and I am constantly developing the ideas presented in this book. Join me on my blog to continue the discussion. I look forward to connecting with you. @ccbakermarriage.com

Epilogue

Remember that Hollywood fairy tale ending I was talking about in Chapter 2? Remember how I thought it would have to be rewritten? It turns out that it didn't need to be rewritten at all. In fact, the love story continued.

Three years after my husband passed, I had yet another blind date and met a dashingly handsome, intellectually stimulating, laughter inducing man who was equally captivated by my four children and me. I resisted him for the longest time and made certain that he understood that under no certain circumstances would we date, marry or procreate. At the time of publishing we are approaching our ten-year wedding anniversary and our child together is nearly eight. He has loved my first four as if they were his own.

None of this would be possible without the ability to remind myself that I CAN be happy. I CAN thrive. I CAN raise a family and have a successful business.

When I became a widow, my proverbial plate became bigger and heavier. All of the responsibility of raising a family was on my shoulders. So many friends and family members offered to help, and while that was so deeply appreciated, ultimately, I knew I had to carry the load. I planned for our future. I implemented automated systems not only in the household, but also in my professional life, so that the kids and I could have quality time together. I made sure that I took care of myself, so that I had that much more to give.

It is because of all of this that the fairy tale continued. When I met Rob, I was grounded. I was independent. I was whole. I was thriving. I had so much more to offer him as a friend and partner because I had implemented all of these strategies. Success was possible because I believed in the power of I CAN. Happiness was possible again because I set up the opportunity for it and chose to thrive instead of just survive. I couldn't be more blessed to have him in my life and in the lives of my older children. The love story continues as it always does, in the right time.

Appendix

A. I CAN Method

Simplify and remember. YOU **CAN** DO THIS!

I = Initiate Self Care

> Do something consistently that generates new energy in you.

C = Connect

> Consistently and uniquely connect to family, friends, clients and customers.

A = Automate

> Create recurring procedures or structures that will create more time in your home and business life.

N = Navigate to success

> Have a plan. Create an ultimate vision supported by goals and strategies.

B. What Are Your Priorities?

Break the self-sabotage cycle by tracking your hours.

How do you spread out your efforts?

Create a mind map, a bullet journal entry, or use an online app or a sheet of paper and mark down the beginning and end of each activity you partake in. I really do mean every single one. Trust me. The information will be useful. Use my example below as a guideline of what to expect to record. This will be a good visual of what you spend time on.

What you spend time on is what you hold as a priority. For 2-7 days (no less than 2), track how you spend your day. Look at the information and ask yourself some questions.

1. Am I including self-care?

2. How many hours do I actually work? Is it more or less than expected?

3. Are there pockets of time where I am lost in a game or some mindless activity that is not self-care?

4. Am I carving out time to connect with clients, customers, family and/or friends?

Whether you track on paper or using an online app, taking inventory of how much time you put towards work, self-

Appendix

care, with family/friends/customers, playing games, etc., will be helpful in knowing where to shift your attention and energy. Then, and only then, will you be able to skillfully fine-tune your plan, vision and goals, create effective and efficient processes and structures, seek out opportunities for creative connections and schedule self-care appropriately.

C. Resources

I share several complimentary resources on my website such as templates for:

- to do lists

- meal planning

- bullet journaling

Find all of this and more at
http://ccbakermarriage.com/complimentary/

About the Author

Christine Baker Marriage is a strategist, a blogger, an author and a speaker. She has been working with her clients to create balance for nearly 10 years. Whether as a bodyworker or as a strategist, Christine's passion and focus is teaching her clients ways to implement symmetry between work and life.

As a mother of five children and the owner and operator of two successful businesses, Christine is no stranger to time management. At her consulting practice, she prides herself on helping her clients breakthrough stifling obstacles and reach new levels of success both personally and professionally.

You can find Christine on all social media @CCBakerMarriage.

Made in the USA
Middletown, DE
11 June 2017